# animal babies

## in polar lands

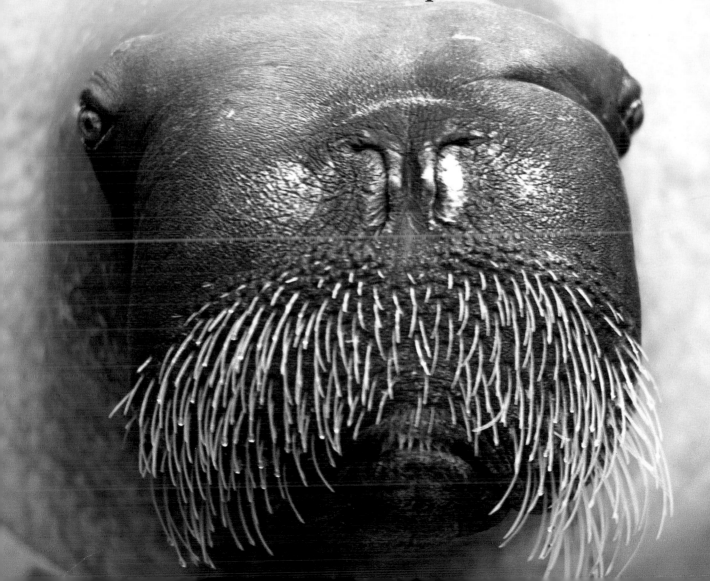

# KINGFISHER

Kingfisher Publications Plc
New Penderel House
283–288 High Holborn
London WC1V 7HZ
www.kingfisherpub.com

First published by Kingfisher Publications Plc 2004
10 9 8 7 6 5 4 3 2

2TR/1204/TWP/PICA(PICA)/150STORA
Copyright © Kingfisher Publications Plc 2004

A CIP catalogue record for this book
is available from the British Library.

ISBN–13: 978 0 7534 0941 1
ISBN–10: 0 7534 0941 0

**Author and Editor:** Jennifer Schofield
**Designer:** Joanne Brown
**Jacket Designer:** Joanne Brown
**Picture Manager:** Cee Weston-Baker
**Picture Researcher:** Rachael Swann
**DTP Manager:** Nicky Studdart
**Senior Production Controller:** Deborah Otter

Printed in Singapore

# animal babies

## in polar lands

I have **flippers** instead of **legs**. They help me to swim very **quickly** in the **cold** water.

*Who is my mummy?*

My mummy
is a harp seal
and I am her pup.

My fur is soft and white, but my mummy's fur is sleek and brown.

I have pointy ears that stand straight up. They help me to hear sounds that are far away.

Who is my mummy?

My mummy is
a wolf and
I am her cub.

I like to
play when it
is sunny, but my
mum likes to rest.

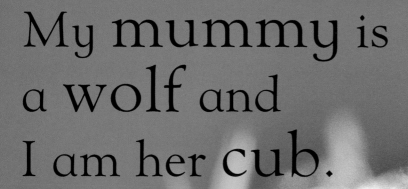

My beak is black and very sharp. I use it to catch fish when I am hungry.

Who is my mummy?

My mummy is an albatross and I am her chick.

I stay in the nest with my mum until I can fly.

I have **pads** under my hooves. They are like snow shoes and **stop** me from slipping on the ice.

*Who is my mummy?*

My **mummy** is a caribou and I am her **calf**.

In the **summer** our **coats** are brown, but in the **winter** they turn **grey**.

I have two big flippers on each side of my body. I use my flippers to dive in and out of the icy water.

Who is my mummy?

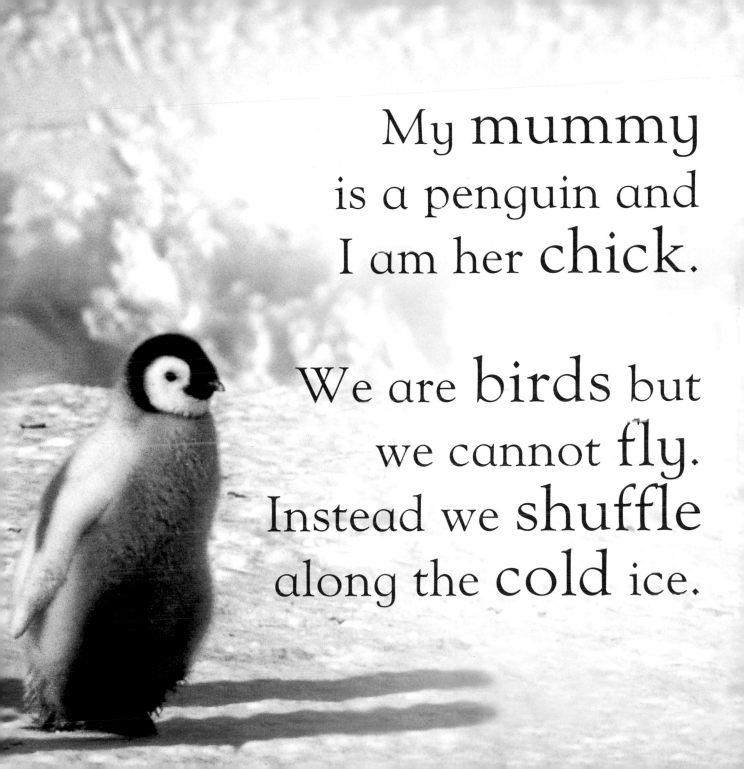

My mummy
is a penguin and
I am her chick.

We are birds but
we cannot fly.
Instead we shuffle
along the cold ice.

I have rows of whiskers
on my chubby face.
They look just like
a moustache.

*Who is my mummy?*

My mummy is
a walrus and
I am her cub.

Our fat keeps
us warm when
it is icy cold.

I am the **biggest** of all the **polar** animals. I have thick **white** fur that keeps me **warm**.

*Who is my mummy?*

My mummy is a polar bear and I am her cub.

In the winter, we sleep in a den under the snow.

## Additional Information

The earth's polar lands are ice-covered, beautiful and home to a great variety of animals. Many of these animals adapt to ensure their survival in these harsh climatic conditions. For example, polar bears have small ears and tails to ensure a minimal loss of heat. Antarctica, the frozen continent surrounding the earth's South Pole, is home to emperor penguins, the largest species of penguin. Harp seals, wolves, albatrosses, caribou, walruses and polar bears are found in the cold and windy Arctic Circle.

## Acknowledgements

The publisher would like to thank the following for permission to reproduce their material. Every care has been taken to trace copyright holders. However, if there have been unintentional omissions or failure to trace copyright holders, we apologise and will, if informed, endeavour to make corrections in any future edition.

Cover: Frank Lane Picture Agency; Half title: Gunter Marx Photography/Corbis; Title page: Norbert Rosing/National Geographic; Harp seal 1: Frank Lane Picture Agency; Harp seal 2: Norbert Rosing/National Geographic; Wolf 1: Art Wolfe/Getty; Wolf 2: Joel Sartore/National Geographic; Albatross 1: Art Wolfe/Getty; Albatross 2: Edwin Mickleburgh/Ardea; Caribou 1: Bill Bleisch/Ardea; Caribou 2: Paul Nicklen/National Geographic; Penguin 1: Tim Davis/Corbis; Penguin 2: Ardea; Walrus 1: Gunter Marx Photography/Corbis; Walrus 2: Norbert Rosing/National Geographic; Polar bear 1: Oxford Scientific Films; Polar bear 2: Norbert Rosing/National Geographic